SPEAK UP

A Practical Guide in the Elements of Effective Speaking

Nancy N. Dill

VANTAGE PRESS
New York / Los Angeles

FIRST EDITION

Copyright © 1990 by Nancy N. Dill

Published by Vantage Press, Inc.
516 West 34th Street, New York, New York 10001

Manufactured in the United States of America
ISBN: 0-533-08612-4

Library of Congress Catalog Card No.: 89-90356

1 2 3 4 5 6 7 8 9 0

Guide to Being an Effective Speaker

Effective Speaker

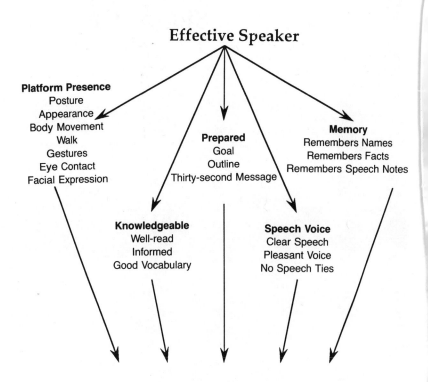

Platform Presence
Posture
Appearance
Body Movement
Walk
Gestures
Eye Contact
Facial Expression

Prepared
Goal
Outline
Thirty-second Message

Memory
Remembers Names
Remembers Facts
Remembers Speech Notes

Knowledgeable
Well-read
Informed
Good Vocabulary

Speech Voice
Clear Speech
Pleasant Voice
No Speech Ties

Self-confident Leader

SPEAK UP

Contents

SPEAK UP

Part One

Fundamentals of Effective Speech

I. Introduction

> Speech is a mirror of the soul; as a man speaks,
> so is he.
> —Publilius Syrus

Reasons for Speech Training

Virtually everyone has far more potential ability than they ever use. In fact, most people have much more capacity for successful achievement than they even recognize. Once they realize the unused talent and ability that is within them, the direction of their lives can change.

Are you a participator or a spectator in life? The ability to speak in public is a basic skill for those who are participators. It distinguishes the leaders from the followers.

We judge people by how they speak as speech is an indication of all that an individual is. You may not be aware of how you sound—but others are.

Equally important is your facility to express yourself physically. Before you say a word you reveal something about yourself by the way you stand, walk, sit, and the expression on your face.

1

Everyone wants to become all that he is capable of becoming. Success in life is becoming what you want to be. You can help others more by making the most of yourself.

Marshall McLuhan's famous assertion that "the medium is the message" applies to speech more than other forms of communication.

How you say something is more important than what you say.

Your speech image can be your greatest asset—or your worst liability.

> Let thy speech be better than silence; or be silent.
> —Dionysius

You—Personal Evaluation

> Are you a princess to look at but a frog to listen to? A tiger to see but a mouse to hear? Is your voice whiny? Nasal? Are you a mumbler?
>
> —Dorothy Sarnoff

Speech blemishes detract from your talk. To eliminate them, first they have to be identified.

Do you have these speech defects?

- nervousness
- nasal or shrill voice
- mumbling
- monotony
- weak voice

Do you pepper your speech with "you knows," "ums," and "ahs?"

The highest and most profitable learning is the knowledge of ourselves.

—Thomas a Kempis

Before you can improve on any problem you have to know what it is. That requires an honest appraisal.

How do you sound? Find out by using a tape recorder.

Look in the mirror to check your posture. You not only look better with good posture, but it's better for your health.

Do you participate well in a social group? Do you contribute your share of the conversation? Do others listen to what you have to say?

All this comes under the heading of self-analysis, which leads to self-knowledge. That is the first step for improved human relations.

Resolve to be thyself: and know that he who finds himself, loses his misery.

—Matthew Arnold

The precept, "know yourself," was not solely intended to obviate the pride of mankind; but likewise that we might understand our own worth.

—Cicero

Aims of this Book

The aims of this book are to guide you in the practical methods of effective communication and to show methods for continual self-development.

When you finish this book you will:

- Become an effective speaker when speaking to one or one hundred.
- Gain a better understanding of yourself and others.
- Develop logical thought processes.
- Develop enthusiasm.
- Become a better listener.
- Improve your articulation and voice.
- Learn how to prepare speeches.
- Improve your memory. Learn how to remember names.
- Improve your phone conversations.
- Get your message across in thirty seconds.
- Overcome nervousness.
- Gain self-confidence.

Effective speaking ability is best achieved through a working knowledge of basic principles and by directed practice.

You will also find that there is nothing that will help you more in acquiring self-confidence than the ability to speak in public. Believe and go to it.

II Stage Fright

I found that learning to speak in public is nature's own method of overcoming self-consciousness and building up courage and self-confidence. Why? Because speaking in public makes us come to grips with our fears.

—Dale Carnegie
The Quick and Easy Way to Effective Speaking

Fear defeats more people than any other one thing in the world.

—Ralph Waldo Emerson

Those Butterflies

Most people have stage fright when they speak in front of a group. They get butterflies in their stomachs, their hands become clammy, their knees are weak and shaky, and they wonder if they're going to faint. It's a ghastly feeling but can be relieved, if not eradicated completely. Many adults enroll in a speech class mainly to conquer that fear.

Why is there such fear? Some reasons are that you're afraid you'll make a fool of yourself, you might forget what you plan to say, what you're saying isn't worthwhile, or that the audience won't like it. But largely a person is fearful because he's more concerned with his own image than his message.

Stage fright can handicap you in your activities if you feel unable or incapable of speaking in public.

Stage fright can be an asset. Like a racehorse a speaker needs to be keyed up and stimulated to do her best. Nervous energy can be directed toward the audience, and you can use your tension to put feeling into your speech. A phlegmatic and casual speaker often is dull and uninteresting. Be glad you have emotions to give you vitality.

Overcoming Stage Fright

The ability to speak effectively is an acquirement rather than a gift.

—William Jennings Bryan

To begin with, look at speaking in public as an opportunity to rise above mediocrity and become a leader. However, a leader is not always a good speaker. But remember anyone can be.

Choose a worthwhile topic that you have earned the right to talk about through experience or research, and most important, that you want to talk about. Speak when you are sure you have something to say, and know just what it is. Then say it and sit down.

There is no substitute for preparation, and good preparation is guaranteed to lessen your anxiety. If you know you have done all you can then your speech is nine tenths delivered.

Practice. But practice correctly. Practice does not make perfect. If you speak often you can usually eliminate nervousness. But without the fundamentals and correct preparation and practice, you will seldom gain proficiency in speaking.

Avoid reading or memorizing a speech except for formal occasions, and rarely then. By reading a speech you are more likely to be jittery because your mind is free to think about yourself as you mechanically read the words, instead of concentrating on your message. You can't think of two things at once. So if you're thinking of your message, you eliminate self-consciousness or awareness of shaky knees.

Also, if you are dependent upon a written speech, you exclude spontaneity. The same thing happens with a memorized speech. But there you have a bigger pitfall— you could forget. An extemporaneous speech (one prepared with notes) is far more effective and interesting than one you read, even if you read well. In addition, it gives you opportunity for direct eye contact with your audience.

Recognize the positive attitude of your audience. They want you to succeed. They don't want to waste their time. Audiences are empathetic and responsive, and are, after all, made up of individuals.

Always keep in mind that public speaking is planned conversation, so you should speak to one hundred people as conversationally as you would to one person.

Gaining Confidence

It would be almost impossible to complete a public speaking course without gaining self-confidence. In fact, that is the most important far-reaching result of a speech course.

If you act confidently you will feel confident. Practice walking and standing with good posture, with your chest and head up. And practice speaking with distinct enunciation and with a well-modulated tone of voice. Confidence is catching. Your message can get across to your audience better if they're comfortable. Besides being prepared, be sure that you're rested and have eaten sufficiently.

Ask yourself what is the worst that could happen. You could forget your speech, but your notes would take care of that. You might be so nervous you wouldn't be able to speak. But think of all the speakers you know who gave excellent talks and confessed afterwards how nervous they were. Often your jitters are known only to you.

Audiences are compassionate. They know that what might happen to the speaker could happen to them. Think of your past experiences when you spoke in class or at social engagements. Lastly, no matter what, how you deliver your speech will not be the end of the world. Relatively speaking, your speech is really a trivial matter, though not to you.

One assured way of overcoming undue nervousness is to speak as often as you can. Make announcements; speak up at meetings and in class. Be sure you have something pertinent to say and you get your point across in thirty seconds or less. Grab hold of any opportunity that comes your way to speak. Once you have established a reputation for speaking well you will find yourself in demand as a speaker.

> There is no other accomplishment, which any man can have which will so quickly make for him a career and secure recognition as the abilty to speak acceptably.
> —Chauncey M. Depew

III. Your Goals

There is only one thing that will train the human mind and that is the voluntary use of the mind by the man himself. You may aid him, you may guide him, you may suggest to him, but above all else you may inspire him: but the only thing worth having is that which he gets by his own exertions and what he gets is in direct proportion to what he puts into it.

—Dr. A. Lawrence Lowell

Motivation

Psychologists claim that there can be no real learning without motivation. Motivation comes from the Latin word *movere* which means "to move." You are moved from where you are now to where you want to be. If you want to be a lawyer or teacher, you are moved to go through the training in order to qualify. The more definite the goal the easier it is to achieve. Goals are the building blocks of motivation. The following is a list of common ones.

- Earn money.
- Build a career.
- Satisfy a desire to know a particular subject.
- Achieve a certain status.
- Compensate for gaps in your early education.
- Be better than the average.

No man can be happy unless he feels his life is in some way important.

—Bertrand Russell

IV. You as Speaker

The most important thing in public speaking is the man.

—Henry Ward Beecher

What then, in brief, does a cultivated modern audience demand of a speaker? It insists, first, that the speaker himself be genuine; second, that he know something worthwhile and know it well; third, that his own feelngs and convictions be fully enlisted in the theme that he presents; and forth, that he talk straight to the point in simple, natural forceful language.

—Lockwood-Thorpe

Be Yourself

You are unique. No one is like you now, ever has been, or ever will be. No one says the same thing in the same way. It's your individuality that will develop as you progress, and you will become free to be yourself without fear or self-consciousness.

A well-designed window lets in light, but does not call attention to itself; nor should a speaker. One of the aims of this book is for the student to gain the capacity to be natural in speaking situations. The problem is not one of superimposing additional characteristics, but rather one of removing impediments and freeing you to speak with naturalness. It takes training, hard work and experience for an actor to be natural and believable on stage and not give the impression he's acting. The same principle applies to a public speaker. Emerson wrote, "Use what language you will, you can never say anything but what you are."

A speaker's character may be called the most effective means of persuasion he possesses.

What we are speaks more loudly than what we say.

Personality (Ethos)

Elbert Hubbard said, "Personality—with the exception of preparation—is probably the most important factor in public address. In eloquent speaking it is the manner that wins, not the word." Aristotle claimed that a speaker's total personality, which he called ethos, consists of three components: intelligence, integrity and goodwill.

Intelligence

To Aristotle intelligence meant not only the raw brainpower you were born with, but also all that you have learned since from experience, your knowledge and skills, and most important the ability to keep on learning. Your background is the basis for any speech preparation. You may be asked to give an impromptu talk on your home town. Even though an impromptu talk is unprepared in organization, your background provides the necessary information.

Everything you learn becomes part of your background, which is broadened by extensive reading. Francis Bacon once said, "Reading makes a full man; conference [speech] a ready man, and writing an exact man."

What you learn should be the basis for intelligent

reasoning. Robert M. LaFollett, a former Governor and Senator, told an audience, "In this country of ours, no man's opinions are worth a whit more than the reasons which are behind them." Robert G. Ingersoll, a lawyer and eloquent public speaker, said almost the same thing, "Back of the art of speaking must be the power to think. Without thought, words are empty purses."

Integrity

The second element of ethos is integrity. If a judge has been accused of conflict of interests, then his speaking on the number of corrupt politicians in government is meaningless. A movie actor once did a television commercial stating why people should quit smoking. When he was subsequently arrested in Europe for possession of marijuana, not surprisingly, his commercial was quickly canceled.

One student gave an impressive talk to his school until a teacher realized that his information came verbatim from *Time* Magazine. His speech was negated by his loss of integrity. Always give credit for material you use. Moreover, your words have more validity if you can substantiate your theme with quotes from an expert. In Mark Twain's autobiography he tells numerous stories about the effect of a person's reputation on his effectiveness as a speaker. William Hazlitt said, "Honesty is one part of eloquence; we persuade others by being in earnest ourselves."

Goodwill

According to Aristotle, the third component of ethos is goodwill, or attitude. What is your attitude toward your audience? Do you feel strongly enough about your subject to want to inform or persuade them? Do you care about their reaction to you? The audience determines the end and the object of your speech.

Politicans who give basically the same speeches know the value of varying the content with each vicinity. In other words, they would emphasize different needs to people in New York City than to the inhabitants of Caribou, Maine.

Popular lecturers make a point of finding out as much as possible about their audiences before speaking. Nothing warms an audience more than to have a speaker open his talk with some fact or feature that is pertinent to them.

Find out as much as you can about your audience and adjust your talk accordingly. Learn what their interests and concerns are. If you were talking at a PTA meeting you would recognize their primary concern with their children's welfare. If you were speaking to senior citizens you would discuss the values of old age and remedies for their well-being. That principle applies in your relationships with other individuals as you adapt your conversation to your listener's interest.

Enthusiasm

If you gain nothing more from this book than an awareness of the power of enthusiasm, you will have gained a great deal. The definition of *enthusiasm* is "ardent zeal, interest, and fervor (intensity of expression)." It comes from two Greek words, *en*, meaning "in," and *theos*, meaning God. So literally *enthusiasm* means "God in us."

Enthusiasm cannot be simulated or superficial, but must be sincere. It means taking an interest in something that absorbs you. By radiating vitality and animation, you draw your audience to you. Russell H. Conwell wrote, "Be intensely in earnest. Enthusiasm invites enthusiasm."

If two people apply for the same job, the one with enthusiasm will have a better chance of getting hired even over one with better credentials. A person who is interested in his job will work harder than one who has a perfunctory attitude. The one who watches the clock and leaves promptly at five will not advance far.

Frederick Williamson, one time president of the New York Central Railroad said "The longer I live, the more certain I am that enthusiasm is the little-recognized secret of success. The difference in actual skill and ability and intelligence, between those who succeed and those who fail, is usually neither wide nor striking. But if two men are nearly equally matched, the man who is enthusiastic will find the scales tipped in his favor. And a man of second-rate ability with enthusiasm will often outstrip one of first-rate ability without enthusiasm."

When Sir Edward Victor Appleton, physicist and Nobel Prize winner, was asked if he had any recipe for success, he said, "Yes, enthusiasm, I rate that even ahead of professional skill."

It doesn't matter what you are interested in, as long as you have an interest in something.

Suppose you're not particularly interested in much of anything. Then bear in mind that the more you know about something and the more skillful you become at something, the more enthusiastic you will be.

Look, act, and feel enthusiastic and you will become enthusiastic. Read the following quotations out loud with enthusiasm.

I like the man who bubbles over with enthusiasm. Better be a geyser than a mud puddle.

—John G. Shedd,
former president of Marshall Field and Co.

Merit begets confidence, confidence begets enthusiasm, enthusiasm conquers the world.

—Walter H. Cottinham,
past president of Sherwin Williams Co.

In the last analysis, all art is autobiographical. You can sing only what you are. You can paint only what you are. You can write only what you are. You can speak only what you are. You must be what your experiences, your environment and your heredity have made you. For better or for worse, you must play your own little instrument in the orchestra of life.

—Dale Carnegie

There is a time in every man's education when he arrives at the conviction that envy is ignorance, that imitation is suicide; that he must take himself for better, for worse, as his portion; that though the wide universe is full of good, no kernel of nourishing corn can come to him but through his toil bestowed on that plot of ground which is given him to till. The power which resides in him is new in nature, and none but he knows what that is which he can do, nor does he know until he has tried.

—Emerson

V. Preparation

The best way for you to gain confidence is to prepare so well on something that you really want to say that there can be little chance to fail.

—Lockwood-Thorpe

O trust to the inspiration of the moment—that is the fatal phrase upon which many promising careers have been wrecked. The surest road to inspiration is preparation. I have seen many men of courage and capacity fail for lack of industry. Mastery in speech can only be reached by mastery in one's subject.

—Lloyd George

Steps in Preparing a Speech

To prepare your speech, first, decide your purpose; second, select your topic; third, gather and organize your material; fourth, make an outline, and fifth, practice.

Speech Purposes

In general your speech purpose will be to inform or to persuade, and sometimes a combination of both. Decide what you want to accomplish with your talk. Then select your topic.

Topics

"I don't know what to talk about," is a common cry of beginning speech students. The first thing to do is to look inward. Start thinking about your experiences and the people you've met, and you'll notice how ideas generate.

But what is vital is your interest in your topic plus your desire to talk about it. And most important, you must have earned the right to talk about it, either through experience or research. If you talk about a magazine article, include your opinion which is what counts. After all, we can read the article for ourselves.

Another thing to bear in mind in your search for material is the fact that people are interested in people. The front pages of newspapers are filled with human interest stories; articles about people who make news sell magazines.

Research

In order to be qualified to speak on your chosen topic, you must have done some research or have experience.

Before you start on your research make a list of what you know, and then make a list of what you need to know. Talk to others who know more about the subject than you and go to the library and look up your topic. The *Reader's Guide to Periodical Literature* is helpful for information for your speeches. However, speaking from your own experience carries the most conviction.

Gathering and Organizing Your Material

If you're doing research, know exactly what you're looking for and learn where to look. Have your theme firmly in mind and know what your main ideas are, then arrange them so one leads into another in a steady progression.

Pare your material down so that your speech will take

no longer than two minutes for two reasons. One, you will have to stick to the point, and two, because of limited time. You can say a lot in two minutes. Notice how much news is covered in a five-minute broadcast. By sticking to a time limit, you will have to think clearly and concisely. Actually thirty seconds is long enough to say what you want to say and to grab and hold your listeners' attention.

Thirty seconds is long enough to persuade or convince your listeners and to make any point you want to make and make it effectively. If you have five minutes or five hours, when the time comes to make your point make it in thirty seconds. The heart of the matter should be said in thirty seconds.

When you prepare your thirty-second message, you'll be able to focus your thinking, writing and speaking. (Read *How to Get Your Point Across in 30 Seconds or Less,* by Milo O. Frank.)

The Outline

Your outline is like a road map. No traveler would start on a cross-country trip without a map if he wanted to be sure of his destination. Nor would a builder erect a house without a blueprint. And no speech should be prepared without an outline.

As long as your outline has a framework with an opening, a middle, and a conclusion, your organization can be flexible to suit your needs.

The Opening or Hook

Your opening sentence, or hook, should get your listeners' immediate attention, just as the first sentence of an article catches the reader's interest so he'll read further. It should lead into the body of the speech.

The hook is what makes you remember, buy a product, stay tuned to a show, or keep reading a book. Headlines in the newspapers are hooks. Commercials use hooks with their thirty-second messages. A hook is a statement or an object used specifically to get attention.

Your hook could be the thesis or reason for your talk. Or that could come later and you could start off with an anecdote or dialogue to arouse interest.

The Body of the Speech

The body (or middle) is the main part of the speech and can include examples, facts, statistics, anecdotes, illustrations, dialogue, or any means that clarify your theme.

Conclusion

The conclusion is often a summary of the speech and sometimes refers back to the opening. Your conclusion can call for specific action, and with a relevant quote, tell a story that echoes the speech, reiterate the point, question or challenge your audience or make an appeal.

The Importance of the Opening and Closing

The opening and the closing are the most important parts of your speech because the opening arouses interest and the closing leaves the last impression.

Write out and memorize your opening and closing sentences, but the rest of your speech should consist of headings and subheadings. By memorizing your opening sentence you are able to launch right into your speech and avoid the "Ums," "ahs," "you knows," and other irrelevancies, which interfere with your communication.

With a memorized ending, you know just what to say and can end on a firm note.

One more reason to memorize these two sentences is to give you the opportunity to look directly at your audience instead of your notes. However, never memorize anything else except a quotation or something that requires accuracy.

Practice

Practice out loud either by yourself or with a friend. Stand the way you will when you actually deliver your speech with correct platform presence. Keep your weight evenly distributed and your feet firmly on the floor with one foot slightly ahead of the other. Keep your hands at your sides. That is the natural position for them even if you feel unnatural. This frees your hands to make gestures. You lack poise if you keep your hands behind your back, folded over your stomach, or in your pockets or, worse yet, if you cross your arms over your chest. All these postures reveal something about you; mainly, that you lack poise. There is a correlation between a speaker's posture and audience attention.

The problem of what to do with your hands is a common one which happens to most people. Keep them at your sides and feel free to use them to express yourself.

Don't practice by looking in a mirror because then you will be more concerned with your image than your message.

Concentrate on speaking clearly.

If you follow the methods outlined and practice, you're on your way to becoming an effective speaker.

Introducing a Speaker

Introducing a speaker involves the same principle as an introduction of one person to another. Your purpose in introducing a speaker is to give the audience information about him and his subject to help establish a link between speaker and audience.

An introduction should be short—sixty seconds or less. The more important the speaker, the shorter the introduction should be. If he's important the audience will know about him, and it's insulting to assume they don't.

Be brief and keep to the following guide.

- State the topic.
- State why the topic is important.
- Give facts about the speaker. Give his name last.

When you announce the name (the very last part of your introduction) speak it clearly and enthusiastically.

Always check beforehand with the speaker about what facts he would like included in his introduction.

Avoid clichés, such as: "It is my pleasure," "Without further ado," "I have the honor," or "I now give you." In fact, avoid overused sayings anyway. Reactivate your thinking with new words.

Basically, the test of a good introduction is the eagerness with which the audience anticipates the speech.

VI. Delivery

Before Your Talk

Walk to the front of the room firmly and confidently. Look at your audience before you speak. Think of your speech as a chance to share what you know with others.

Physical Movement

Some physical movement not only keeps your audience's attention but also uses up nervous energy. When you make a movement complete it. If you point, use your whole arm, not just your hand. Movements should be definite, not halfhearted gestures. Remember they emphasize and enhance your speech and give you vitality. Become aware of how much is conveyed through body language.

After Your Talk

Keep direct eye contact with all members of your audience. Stay in place until you've finished the last word and then confidently go back to your seat. If you have done the best you can, you have every right to feel confident because no one can ask more of you than that.

Audience

Always relate your subject to your audience. If it interests you, it probably will interest others. Ask yourself

why it appeals to you and why it might to others. Then
mention it. In your conclusion show how your talk might
be useful to them. Plan your introduction and conclusion
last.

Visual Aids

The most important thing to remember is that nothing
should interfere with your communication. If you pass
exhibits around during your talk, you'll lose your audience's attention. A visual aid is just an aid and should not
take precedence over your words.

An exhibit by itself has limited value. So don't give it
more attention than your listeners. Use it only when you
need it. Beware of individual demonstrations or turning
your back on half the group to explain or demonstrate to
the other half.

If you turn your back to write on a blackboard or set
up your exhibit, explain what you are doing. Silence can
lose your audience. Lastly, keep your aids out of sight until
you need them. If you don't, they could become objects of
curiosity and of more interest than your words. Put them
aside when you're through with them.

Practice exactly as you plan to deliver your speech.
Plan how you're going to arrange your aids. If you need
a table or blackboard make sure it's there. And practice
out loud.

Telling a Story

When telling a story be as conversational to a group
of one hundred as you would be to one. Along with speaking naturally and conversationally, make sure you can be
heard and understood.

Microphones

A microphone tends to blur voices and unless you speak clearly don't use one. Anyone who speaks in public should strive for a good voice and clear speech. A microphone can also interfere with your communication because you depend on it and it inhibits your movement. If you do have to use one, at least practice with it first.

Additional Points

- Walk up and back to your seat confidently.
- Be friendly and enthusiastic. Smile.
- Speak distinctly.
- Emphasize important points with vocal inflections, gestures, and movement.
- Memorize your opening and closing sentences and deliver them with conviction.
- Maintain good eye contact.
- Prepare ahead if you use visual aids. If you quote from a book and need to read from it, look up after every few sentences. Don't pick up your book until you use it.
- Don't pass anything out until the end of your speech.

Creating an Emotional Impact—a Way to Successful Speaking

Not all successful speakers have good voices, use correct grammar, use appropriate gestures, are well groomed, or have a good education.

Yet they have one essential ingredient for successful speaking—they are deeply stirred by something.

Speakers who feel strongly about an issue can speak effectively and move their listeners. Often their concern for the message overcomes any inherent speech problems. It's not only their feeling that's transmitted, but also their desire to communicate. If someone or something stirs you deeply, don't you want to talk about it? And you probably would discover that you had no trouble finding the words to express yourself.

Elbert Hubbard was a magazine publisher who was aroused because he felt that people had little loyalty, enthusiasm, or initiative. He poured out his feelings in a short article called "Message to Garcia" that eventually sold forty million copies.

A way to successful speaking is to speak with feeling. Then your delivery will take care of itself.

Part Two

Human Relations

VII. Getting Along with Others

A survey was made by the University of Chicago, the American Association for Adult Education, and the United YMCA schools to determine what adults really want to study. The survey revealed that after health, adults' primary interest is the desire to develop skill in human relationships. In other words they want to know how to get along with people.

Andrew Carnegie paid Charles Schwab a salary of a million dollars a year that Mr. Schwab attributed more to his ability to get along with people than his business acumen. He said, "I consider my ability to arouse enthusiasm among men the greatest asset I possess, and the way to develop the best that is in a man is by appreciation and encouragement. Th re is nothing else that so kills the ambitions of a man as criticisms from his superiors. I never criticize anyone. I believe in giving a man incentive to work. So I am anxious to praise but loathe to find fault. If I like anything, I am hearty in my approbation and lavish in my praise."

Your First Impression

Before you deliver a speech, smile. It's no less important in your daily life. So if you don't feel like smiling, make yourself smile; force the corners of your lips up, sing or hum, and you will find you feel like smiling.

Prof. William James of Harvard put it this way, "Action seems to follow feeling, but really action and feeling go together; and by regulating the action, which is under the direct control of the will, we can indirectly regulate the feeling, which is not."

If you act confidently, you will find yourself thinking in a confident way. We are what we think. "Nothing is good or bad," wrote Shakespeare, "but thinking makes it so."

Abraham Lincoln once remarked, "Most folks are about as happy as they make up their minds to be."

Everyone wants happiness, but happiness depends on inner conditions. James Allen wrote in his inspiring short book *As a Man Thinketh*: "Circumstance doesn't change a man, it reveals him to himself."

Ann Landers wrote once that we can't prevent swallows from flying over our heads, but we can keep them from making a nest there.

James Allen also likened thoughts to a garden. You have to cultivate your thoughts the same way you tend your garden, weeding out the negative thoughts and letting the positive ones grow and strengthen.

William James said, "The greatest discovery of my generation is that human beings can alter their lives by altering their attitudes of mind."

How to Remember Names

In dealing with others you first have to bring out the best in yourself.

The first step in dealing successfully with someone else is to make a point of calling him by name. As Dale Carnegie said, the sweetest sound to anyone is his name.

Make a point of remembering names.

When you are introducing someone make sure you hear the speaker's name correctly, even if you have to ask how it's spelled. No one will mind if you take an interest in his name; on the contrary, he'll be flattered in your interest. Impress his name upon your mind, then associate it with a mental picture with something or someone familiar to you, then repeat it as often as possible.

For example, take the name Dill. You are introduced to Mrs. Dill. Be sure you get it accurately, not Bill or Fill, but Dill. You will probably immediately associate the name with a pickle, then repeat her name when you see her so you won't forget. Common names like Mary, Jane, Nancy, and Susan are the hardest to remember. But if you already know a girl named Susan then associate a new acquaintance with the girl you know. Remember it's very flattering to have your name remembered, and you will find that people will respond to you more warmly when you use their name.

In his book *How to Win Friends and Influence People*, Dale Carnegie summed up rules for effective human relations in a nutshell as follows:

- Become genuinely interested in other people.
- Remember that a man's name is to him the sweetest sound in the English language.
- Be a good listener. Encourage others to talk about themselves.
- Talk in terms of the other man's interests.
- Make the other person feel important and do it sincerely.
- The only way to get the best of an argument is to avoid it.
- Show respect for the other man's opinions. Never tell a man he is wrong.
- If you are wrong, admit it quickly and emphatically.
- Try honestly to see things from the other person's point of view.

Listening

Listen selectively, purposely, actively.

Listening means more than just hearing; it's necessary to listen selectively. Listen to others as you would like them to listen to you.

Good listening requires listening for a purpose.

Listening is just as active as speaking and in some ways more so. The speaker knows what he's going to say, but the listener has to understand the message as it progresses.

Reading and Listening

The process involved in competent reading applies to listening. To read effectively you must also identify the purpose and the main ideas, be aware of the significant details, note the organization of ideas and understand the words. When you're listening you can't go back if you missed something or look ahead.

In listening you have the advantage of hearing the tone of voice and inflections, plus you can see the gestures and facial expressions that add to the meaning of the words.

Both worthwhile listening and reading require active participation. As you can think three times as fast as a speaker can talk, use the spare time to look for answers to questions and to listen critically.

Listen Critically

When you listen critically you evaluate the logic of the speaker's remarks, and if they are valid and backed up by specific examples or facts.

John Stuart Mill wrote the following on critical listening: "Not the violent conflict between parts of the truth, but the quiet suppression of half of it, is the formidable evil; there is always hope when people are forced to listen to both sides; it's when they attend only to one that errors harden into prejudices, and truth itself ceases to have the effect of truth, by being exaggerated into falsehood."

Listen Creatively

When you listen creatively you utilize your own ideas and knowledge. You are creative when you use the comments you hear as springboards for your own ideas.

By listening creatively you add to your own enjoyment and that of the speaker, who gets feedback from his audience. A speaker can feel the response of the audience.

Another thing to note is the speaker's viewpoint and if his opinions are valid, then apply this to yourself. Everything you learn from listening (or reading) should have value for you and should be applicable to you in some way.

Generally, you listen and read to gain knowledge and to increase your understanding so that you can function to the best of your ability and live up to your potential. William James said, "What we do, compared to what we can do, is like comparing the top of the ocean to its mighty depths."

Inattention is the main reason we remember only twenty percent of what we hear.

How to Improve Your Listening

Knowing why you have to listen will help you in your ability to listen skillfully. It also requires conscientious practice like anything else. You can play tennis or the piano for years with little improvement if you don't practice with a determined effort to improve.

One last thing to think of is that attentive listening is also a form of courtesy. Give the same attention to others that you would want for yourself. Give the speaker your visual attention as well. Leave your knitting or sewing behind. Also, as you know, you learn almost as much from a person's delivery, his facial expression, and body movements as you do from his words.

Importance of Words

The following quotation highlights the importance of words. Another reason we should learn to listen.

Soft words sung in a lullaby will put a babe to sleep. Excited words will stir a mob to violence. Eloquent words will send armies marching into the face of death. Encouraging words will fan to flame the genius of a Rembrandt or a Lincoln. Powerful words will mold the public mind as the sculptor molds his clay. Words, spoken or written, are a dynamic force.

—Wilfred Peterson

VIII.   Conversation

A single conversation across the table with a wise
man is worth a month's study of books.
—Chinese proverb

The Value of Conversation

Men have extolled the value of conversation since ancient
times. "It is good to rub and polish our brain against that
of others," wrote the French essayist Michel de Montaigne.

"I attribute the little I know to my not having been
ashamed to ask for information and to my rule of convers-
ing with all descriptions of men on those topics that form
their own peculiar professions and pursuits," wrote the
English philosopher John Locke.

Good conversation can be stimulating, bring you closer
to others, increase your knowledge of yourself and others,
add to your information, give you pleasure, help you solve
problems and clear up misunderstandings.

Ways to Become a Good Conversationalist

Perhaps you feel that you have nothing to say. Those
who participate most are well informed and want to share
their ideas and convictions. Your ideas develop through
verbal exchange.

Remember that you have a right to your opinion, and if you feel that you have nothing pertinent to add to a discussion, then ask questions so that you will learn more.

One guaranteed way to help you communicate with people, even strangers, is to smile. It's hard not to respond to a smile. It establishes a warm relationship and adds to your attractiveness. It also gives your voice a better tone. Think of the telephone company's slogan, "The voice with the smile."

Conversation is a two-way street; it takes two people, a speaker and a listener, as in tennis where it takes one to hit the ball and one to return it. The ball should be kept in play as in conversation. If you want to avoid dead-end answers (no, yes, maybe) phrase your questions so they require an answer, such as: "why would you"—"what do you think about"—"in your opinion"—"how did you"—"can you explain"—or "can you give me an example." How, what, and why are good conversational openers.

Stick to the Point

"I don't know if it's going to snow tomorrow, of course, I might not be able to get the car—Charlie might take it, but if it does snow he might take a ride with Art because he has a Jeep and I'm not sure if John's cold will be better. If it's not, I suppose I better stay home. It's terribly early, but could you play tennis at 9:00 tomorrow?" That speaker is a rambler; she doesn't stick to the point but fills her conversation with irrelevancies.

Rambling indicates a vague way of thinking, and indeed she was thinking out loud. In a case like that, often one idea makes a person think of another and still another until she's suddenly forgotten what she started out to say.

Whether you are addressing thousands or talking to one person, come to the point and stay with it.

Telephoning

If you phone busy people it helps to think what you're going to say beforehand. Get your thoughts formulated to avoid needless digressions and repetitions. By organizing your speeches you will find your daily conversation also more organized, because you'll be thinking in a more coordinated way.

Avoid the Word I

A bore is a person who monopolizes the conversation with anecdotes about himself or family. Instead of saying, "What I think. . . . " ask, "What do you think?" If you sense that you have been talking more than others then toss the conversational ball to someone else. Take your cue from the way your listeners look—are they attentive. If you don't give your listeners a chance to verbally respond to you, you can be reasonably sure you haven't gotten their interest.

Avoid "You Know"

Prevalent in today's speech are the meaningless words "you know" with which educators, TV personalities, lecturers, and students, among others, pepper their sentences. These two words have little meaning and even less substance. They are expletives and interjections that may mask nerves, signal boredom, or indicate the extreme inarticulateness of the speaker. They are also annoying obstacles to effective communication.

Listening

Plutarch said, "Know how to listen, and you can learn from those who speak badly." As listening is half of conversation it is equally important. It's a compliment to a speaker to have an attentive listener. Dorothy Sarnoff expressed what the art of conversation was in her book *Speech Can Change Your Life* when she wrote: "It is part of the greater art of leading your life with grace, with charm and with love." This is summed up in the following quotation from the Book of Maccabees.

- Do more than exist—live.
- Do more than look—observe.
- Do more than read—absorb.
- Do more than hear—listen.
- Do more than listen—understand.
- Do more than think—ponder.
- Do more than plan—act.
- Do more than talk—say something.

Additional Points

Topics to Avoid

If you want to bore people, you will succeed if you talk about dogs, children, recipes, domestic problems, and your health. Once an ambassador said to Winston Churchill, "You know, Sir Winston, I've never told you about my grandchildren." Churchill clapped him on the back and exclaimed, "I realize it, my dear fellow, and I can't tell you how grateful I am!"

Avoid Arguing

Direct yourself to the issue rather than to your own emotions or prejudices. Quarreling divides people; discussions bring them together.

Include Others

Don't be so absorbed in your conversation that you forget to include others. If you're having a discussion and one person is silent, draw him/her into the conversation.

Interrupting

John Locke said, "There cannot be a greater rudeness than to interrupt another in the current of his discourse." This may be hard to avoid if you want to insert an opinion or clear up a point or ask a question. Nevertheless, when you do enter the conversation be sure not to interrupt.

Prevalent Grammatical Errors

Examples

Him and his sister went to Iowa City.
(He)

Me and Susan plan to go.
(Susan and I)

Between you and I.
                    (me)

There's lots of them.
(There are)

There wasn't many people there.
            (weren't)

This is her.
        (she)

It's me. (This is okay)

I am far better than him.
                    (he)

Understanding the Process of Communication

Communication is the act of sending ideas and feelings in such a way that the receiver can recreate those ideas and feelings for himself. Communication includes the sender, the message, and the receiver. I cannot communicate in an empty room, any more than I could communicate if no one listened. In the process of communicating the sender opens up new horizons and responsibilities and clarifies his ideas, while the listener acquires information and understanding.

Communication is the central process in cultural diffusion (art, music, literature, drama, dance). It is the most important factor affecting our interpersonal relations, and is a learned activity and, therefore, can be improved.

A breakdown in communication can occur when the sender does the following:

- Assumes the listener knows what he knows.
- Does not have a clear purpose.
- Has incoherent organization.
- Uses words that are not clear.

As the listener is an equal partner, he could be responsible for breakdowns by:

- Being bored or preoccupied.
- Feeling he knows the message so doesn't listen.
- Being opposed to the message.
- Letting his own prejudices interfere with the understanding of the speaker.

Part Three

Communicating Physically

> Action is eloquence, and the eyes of the ignorant
> are more learned than their ears.
>
> —Shakespeare

IX. Platform Presence

Body Language

Body language and spoken language are dependent on each other. You cannot get the complete meaning from the words alone any more than you can from body language alone. To be an integrated person you need to make sure that what you say matches what you do. Therefore, your platform presence and body movement merit as much care and practice as your speech. This also, of course, carries over into your daily life.

Before You Speak

You, the speaker, are judged before you open your mouth. You reveal yourself in the way you walk to the speaker's area and the way you stand when you get there. You convey your attitude and your personality through your body movements.

Choose something worthwhile to say so you will want to talk about it and that will enable you to walk to the front of the room purposely. Your walk will show a person who knows where he is going and why.

And remember to smile. A smile says that you're glad to be there and your audience will respond to you and welcome you. Professor Overstreet in *Influencing Human Behavior* said: "Like begets like." If you show goodwill and enthusiasm your audience will respond in kind.

Lastly, start your speech only when you have everyone's attention.

The Audience

An audience should be crowded together to respond. A scattered audience isn't moved as easily as one packed together where people can lose their identity and be more easily swayed than if they sat surrounded by empty seats. If the hall is only half full, have everyone move down to fill the first half. It's difficult to communicate to a group when you're separated by empty space.

Henry Ward Beecher said in his Yale Lectures on Preaching: "People often say, 'Do you not think it is much more inspiring to speak to a large audience than a small one?' No, I say: I can speak just as well to twelve persons as to a thousand, provided those twelve are crowded around me and close together, so that they can touch each other. But even a thousand people with four feet of space between every two of them, would be just the same as an empty room . . . Crowd your audience together and you will set them off with half the effort."

Adequate Light

It's no less important for a speaker to have adequate lighting than it is for actors on stage. The purpose is to be seen, because as it's been pointed out, your expression and body movement conveys your meaning as much as your words.

Where to Stand and Sit

Just as you need to be seen with sufficient light, you also need to face your audience with nothing blocking their view of you. As tempting as it may be, don't stand behind a table or lectern, because then you lessen your communication effectiveness by hiding three-quarters of your body. Formal occasions, however, necessitate the use of a lectern.

If you're speaking in front of a small group, stand on the same level with them as long as you can be seen and heard. In a panel discussion, be sure the panelists can be seen by more than just the ones in the first few rows. It can be extremely frustrating to hear many speakers and not be able to see them or distinguish between their voices.

If possible avoid having others on the platform with you as that diverts attention from you. Eyes tend to follow any moving thing or person and it's impossible to expect those behind you not to move. No matter how stimulating a speaker is, if someone gets up to shut a door or get to a seat, all eyes will turn in that direction, and the speaker might as well stop and wait until he can recapture the audience's attention.

When sitting on a platform sit straight with your feet flat on the floor with one foot slightly ahead of the other.

This may seem insignificant but when you're on stage everything about you is magnified. Also, never cross your legs, it gives your body a bad line. Your lower back should touch the back of your chair. And look attentive! The spotlight might just be on you.

Appearance

Dress appropriately and comfortably. Check your appearance beforehand so you don't have to think about it. If you know you look your best it will give you more confidence.

Gestures

Gestures should never be planned, but they should naturally follow your thoughts. With your hands at your sides you will have freedom to use them. If you're gripping a lectern or dependent on a microphone you limit your ability to express yourself physically. Every movement that does not add to your presence diminishes it.

Herbert Spencer wrote:

> How truly language must be regarded as a hindrance to thought, though the necessary instrument of it. We shall clearly perceive on remembering the comparative force with which simple ideas are communicated by signs. Today "leave the room" is less impressive than to point to the door. Placing the finger on the lips is more forcible than whispering, "Do not speak." A beck of the hand is better than "come here." No phrase can convey the idea of surprise so vividly as opening the eyes and raising the eyebrows. A shrug of the shoulders would lose much by translation into words.

Posture and Personality

There is a distinct relationship between posture, voice, and personality. Good speech and voice are dependent on good posture and the way you stand, sit, and walk is fundamental for your health and appearance. Katherine Anne Ommanney wrote in *The Stage and the School* that "a slovenly walk, a rigid or slouching posture, irritatingly aimless gestures, or a wooden face reveal our personality just as clearly as do purposeful, vigorous movement and a radiant, mobile face. Nine times out of ten, the world will take you at your 'face value.' "

You are judged first by your appearance and manner, and then by what you say and how you say it.

Posture

Good posture is a major key to beauty and health, and compensates for any other physical imperfections. It includes holding your chest high, your head erect, your shoulders relaxed but properly placed, stomach in and weight evenly distributed. Good posture shows vitality, self-confidence and an interest in yourself and others.

Bad posture includes rounded shoulders, a sunken chest, protruding abdomen, and swayback and usually indicates uneven distribution of weight, which results in lopsided appearance, and gives the impression you lack self-esteem.

Look in the mirror and take an assessment of your body. No matter what your figure is like, correct posture will improve it and poor posture will accentuate the bad points.

How to Check Proper Posture

Lie flat on the floor. Put your hand under your back by your waist. Then lift your knees slightly until your back is pressed firmly against your hand. To counteract a sway back flex your knees slightly.

Now stand against the wall in the same alignment. Keep your heels, your back, your shoulders, and the back of your head against the wall exactly as you were on the floor. Now come away from the wall and stand in the same way to achieve correct posture.

You may feel unnatural at first but your appearance will improve. Practice until it becomes second nature to you and you don't have to think about it. The road to self-knowledge leads to the ability to forget yourself. To get rid of self-consciousness it's necessary to go through a period of self-awareness.

Joseph Conrad said, "No man ever understands quite his own artful dodges to escape from the grim shadow of self-knowledge." But instead of a grim shadow it can be an illuminating experience when you consider the remarkable results.

Motivation

To provide motivation ask yourself two questions: What do I want to do in life that depends on my appearance? Is my present appearance a help or hindrance to me? Then act accordingly.

Voice and Speech

You may wonder how your posture affects your voice and speech. Good voice tone is dependent on proper breathing, and correct diaphragmatic breathing can only be accomplished through good posture. Singers have to develop correct breathing for proper breath control (have you ever seen an opera singer who slumped?), as do actors or anyone who wants to have a strong and resonant voice.

As your attitude is reveaied in your posture, so are your thoughts revealed in your speech. Good voice, speech, and posture go hand in hand.

Part Four

Reading, Vocabulary, and Memory Improvement

X. Reading Improvement

Today we need to know more to keep abreast of events and developments, to use what we learn, to explain, predict, make decisions, to inform, and to persuade for personal as well as for common good.

For you to speak cogently and intelligently you need to read. How well do you read now? What is your comprehension rate? Do you find yourself reading an article and then realizing that you haven't any idea of what you read?

By improving your reading ability you will increase your reading enjoyment. You will read and understand more in less time, and will increase your knowledge and improve your communication.

Fast Reading

The faster you read the more likely you are to concentrate. If you are driving along a thruway at the maximum speed limit of sixty-five miles an hour, your concentration is at its peak as opposed to a leisurely Sunday afternoon drive on a country road when your mind has time to wander.

And yet fast reading is valueless if you don't read for meaning and comprehension. The broader your knowledge is the more you will be able to understand the author's thoughts and ideas and relate them to what you already know.

Shortcuts to Newspaper Reading

Few people have the time or the inclination to read everything in the daily newspapers.

By reading the headlines on the first page you'll get a good idea of the major events during the previous twenty-four hour period. If a headline particularly interests you, read the first paragraph of the article, which usually states the main facts of who, what, where, and how. Read on if you want further details.

Editorials are similar in organization to speeches. The first paragraph (the opening) states what the editorial is about, the middle paragraphs (body) include the details and the last paragraph (conclusion) sums up the editorial and states an opinion. So just by reading the first and last paragraphs you can get the essential information.

Reading Selectively and Purposefully

Effective reading is done at different speeds, just as you drive a car at different speeds. If you were reading a text book, your reading speed would be less than if you were reading a novel.

Decide the purpose of your reading. What do you expect to get from it? What was the author's purpose in writing it? As you read keep formulating questions about the material.

Skimming and Scanning

A competent reader knows when, where, and how to scan and skim his reading material.

When you look up a word in the dictionary you're scanning, which means finding specific information. Dr. Johnson said, "Knowledge is of two kinds. We know a subject ourselves or we know where we can find information about it."

Skimming can involve returning to the text to find an answer, a fact, or a name or to verify a point missed in the reading, or it can involve making a survey of your material. To do that, read the table of contents, the introduction, and sometimes the conclusion to know what to look for in your reading.

A key to effective skimming is a clear understanding of the structure of a paragraph. A paragraph contains one main thought or idea that usually comes at the beginning and sometimes at the end. The ability to pick out the topic sentence in paragraphs will improve your reading habits as well as facilitate your ability to skim.

Be aware of how the writing progresses, how one paragraph leads into another with transitional words or phrases such as: *therefore, however, besides, nevertheless, on the other hand, moreover, first, lastly, in addition, another,* et cetera.

Reading, Writing, Speaking, and Listening

Reading, writing, speaking, and listening are integrated skills; as you improve one, you will automatically improve the others. By improving your reading you will improve your organizational ability in your writing and speaking. This affects your listening ability by enabling you to grasp the meaning more easily when you have a thorough understanding of how material, written or verbal, is organized.

XI. Vocabulary Improvement

> Words on the page are like red blood cells in the
> body. Both are carriers. As red corpuscles carry oxy-
> gen to the tissues, so words carry the thought of the
> writer to the mind of the reader.
>
> —Paul D. Leedy

Vocabulary

Increase your vocabulary. A good vocabulary is a prerequis-
ite to reading skill.

According to Norman Lewis in his book *Word Power
Made Easy*, the Human Engineering Laboratory, an institu-
tion that tests people's aptitudes, found that the only common characteristic of successful people is an understanding
of the meaning of words.

Dr. Johnson O'Connor, director of the laboratory,
explained the relationship between vocabulary and success:
"Why do large vocabularies characterize executives and
outstanding men and women in other fields? The final
answer seems to be that words are the instruments by means
of which men and women grasp the thoughts of others
and with which they do much of their own thinking. They
are tools of thought."

Educational research has discovered that a person's
IQ is related to his vocabulary.

By increasing your vocabulary you will improve your
reading, writing, speaking, and listening ability because

you will accumulate words to express yourself clearly and will understand what others say.

Three Vocabularies

We have three vocabularies. Our reading vocabulary is the largest because you can guess the meaning from the context; your writing vocabulary is the second largest because you have time to think about words to express your thoughts; your speaking vocabulary is the smallest. How often do you hear, "I know what I mean but I just don't know how to say it?"

Big versus Little Words

It's not the length of the word that counts. Use a short word in place of a long one whenever you can. After all, the purpose of communication is to be understood, not to show off your knowledge. With many words at your command you often use one in place of many, which enables you to speak and write more coherently. In other words, you are able to express yourself more clearly and concisely with a large vocabulary.

Colin Mares stated in his book *Rapid and Efficient Reading* that "Anyone who knows or even suspects that his vocabulary is weak should regard vocabulary work as a prime essential. 'Work' is probably not the correct word here. 'Interest' is probably better. Learning about words as well as learning words, and thus bettering our powers of communication, is an essential of life. Be word conscious; try to work out the meaning for yourself; use the dictionary properly; read more; read widely, select carefully and develop a self-confidence in tackling 'difficult books.' "

Your Wordrobe

There is no excuse for poverty of language. You can become a millionaire in the field of words by developing your word power. We need words—we think with them. Dr. John Dewey, the great American educator, said, "Thought is impossible without words."

How to Increase Your Vocabulary

1. Buy a vocabulary book. (See bibliography.)
2. Keep a vocabulary notebook.
3. Write definitions, synonyms, and a sentence using the word.
4. Keep a dictionary and a thesaurus handy when reading and writing.

XII. Memory Improvement

One time seeing is worth a thousand times hearing.

—Chinese proverb

Carl Seashore wrote that "The average man does not use above ten percent of his actual inherited capacity for memory. He wastes the ninety percent by violating the natural laws of remembering."

We are visual minded so eye impressions stick. The nerves that lead from the eye to the brain are twenty times as large as those leading from the ear to the brain.

The three natural laws of memory are impression, repetition, and association.

Impression

To get a clear impression, concentrate. Just as cameras can't take pictures in the fog, neither can you remember what isn't clear in your mind. You can't remember a person's name if you don't hear it distinctly in the first place.

Repetition

Repeat what you want to remember. Repeat parts of your speech or what you've heard or read in your conversation. If you want to remember a person's name, use it when you're talking to him.

In memorizing your information (not your speech) it's more effective to repeat your study at intervals than to try to memorize something at one time.

After you learn something you forget as much during the first eight hours as you do during the next thirty days. So just before you give a speech go over your notes.

Association

The secret of a good memory is the secret of forming diverse and multiple associations with every fact you want to remember. Ask why, how, when, where, and who in relation to what you want to remember.

> The man whose acquisitions stick is the man who is always achieving and advancing whilst his neighbors, spending most of their time in relearning what they once knew, but have forgotten, simply hold their own.
>
> —William James

Part Five

Voice and Speech

I believe that people before they graduate or even matriculate, they should learn to speak up, to speak out, to articulate. It befuddles my sense of acoustic to be mumbled at through a potato, be it from Idaho or Aroostook. This word-swallowing, the smuggled mutes and slovenly slurrings can lead to calamitous misunderstanding and errings. . . .

—Ogden Nash

XIII. Articulation

Speech

Poor speech habits are unfortunately common and can mar your communication as well as create an unfavorable impression. Speech blemishes can be a deciding factor when you apply for a job and can hinder your relations with others.

Check your speech with a tape recorder. Can you understand yourself? Or do you mumble? If so, you're not alone. However, it's an unappealing habit that can be corrected with practice.

Mumbling is due mostly to lazy lips, lack of speech training, and sometimes indicates a lack of self-confidence. To help overcome it practice reading aloud, and make sure that you pronounce every syllable and every consonant.

You will of course sound stilted and will probably have to go slowly at first. But it is one way to activate your lips and tongue. And you can get some of your reading done at the same time. In general, poor speech can be attributed to lazy lips and a lazy tongue.

Practice Rules

In your practice remember the following:

- To speak clearly, every word, syllable, and sound should be given its proper form and value.
- Move your lips noticeably.
- Never keep your teeth closed while speaking.
- Develop flexible lips and tongue.

Articulation and enunciation are used interchangeably. But a speech student should know the difference. Articulation is the physical action of the speech organs in making sounds, and enunciation is the audible result of the articulation.

Often the word *diction* is used for either articulation or enunciation, but it literally means your choice of words.

Pronunciation is the conventional method of sounding a word.

The word *elocution* seems to have gone out of style, mainly, I think, because it connotes a stiff, pedantic speech style, whereas today the trend is toward naturalism.

Vowels help make your speech audible. Consonants are speech sounds which interrupt the free flow of breath from the lungs by momentary closing or friction of the lips, tongue, or teeth.

A syllable is a unit of vocal sounding in a vowel and usually contains one vowel sound.

You can dress up at the last minute but dressing up your speech takes time and effort.

Speech Exercises

Practice the following speech exercises.

For Fs and Vs

- Fine feathers make fine birds.
- Four fellows filled bags full of flour.
- Fanny bought fresh fruit from Fred.
- Butterflies fluttered from flower to flower for food.
- Often I felt I would not be able to afford more.
- Avoid even the very appearance of evil.
- Vincent was victorious over the vicious villain.
- Victor varnished the weather vane.
- Eva found a beautiful vine-clad villa.

For the Sound of S

- Amidst the mists and coldest frost with stoutest wrists and loudest boasts he thrusts his fists against the posts and still insists he sees the ghosts.

Tongue Twisters

- Say *toy boat* several times in rapid succession.
- This is the Michigan State Fish Hatchery.

- Build bigger and better rubber baby buggy bumpers.
- Seated on shore, she sees ships with shining sails on the shimmering sea.
- A skunk sat on a stump. The skunk thunk the stump stunk and the stump thunk the skunk stunk. Which stunk, the skunk or the stump?

Exercises for the Development of Flexibility of the Lips

- Mrs. Peck Pigeon is picking for bread
  Bob-bob-bob goes her little round head.
  Tame as a pussy cat in the street.
  Step-step-step go her little red feet.
  With her little red feet and her little round head,
  Mrs. Peck Pigeon goes picking for bread.

- Betty Botta bought some butter,
  But said she this butter's bitter.
  If I put it in my batter
  It will make my batter bitter.
  But a bit of better butter
  Will make my bitter batter better.
  So she bought a better butter
  Better than the bitter butter
  And it made her bitter batter better.
  So t'was better Betty Botta
  Bought a bit of better butter.

- Peter Piper, the pepper picker,
  picked a peck of pickled peppers,
  A peck of pickled peppers did Peter
  Piper, the pepper picker, pick.
  If Peter Piper, the pepper picker,
  picked a peck of pickled peppers,
  where is the peck of pickled peppers
  that Peter Piper, the pepper picker, picked?

Exercises for Developing Flexibility of the Tip of the Tongue

• Theophilus Thistle, the successful thistle sifter, in sifting a sieve full of unsifted thistles, thrust three thousand thistles through the thick of his thumb. See that thou in sifting a sieve full of unsifted thistles, thrust not three thousand thistles through the thick of thy thumb. Success to the successful thistle sifter.

Exercises for Lazy Lips

• Why do wily women win wealth and wed well?
• Wilma worked woefully while Wallace willfully wandered west.
• Weary Willy washes and wipes wet windows while Walter whistles.
• Welcome wagons wound their way westward while warped wheels wobbled weakly.
• Washington was a wizard warrior, his wisdom and wishes worked wonders.
• Women worried when Warsaw's wild, wet winter weather worsened and workers wearied.
• One weeping willow wisp waves wanly in the wind.
• Woolite warrants washing worn, wilted white woolens well.

For practice in *t*s and *d*s say the following combinations several times.

• little—middle
• patter—paddle
• latter—ladder

XIV. Voice

The Mechanics of Voice

The mechanics of voice—breathing and phonating, articulating and resonating—are important because their application is necessary to convey meaning. The characteristics of a good voice may be listed under six Ps: purity of tone, precision, power, pitch, pattern, and pliability.

Your voice shows when you're tired, sick, elated, disgruntled, angry, excited, enthusiastic, depressed, et cetera. In other words, your voice reveals your emotions.

Voice and Breathing

Voice originates from the voice box or larynx, which contains the vocal chords. Voice is breath passing out from the lungs and vibrating the vocal chords on its way through the mouth where it is articulated or shaped to form words in speech or song.

When you're lying flat on the floor you automatically breathe correctly. So practice in that position and take deep breaths. Then in a standing position in front of a mirror, put one hand on your chest and one hand on your diaphragm (the muscle at the lower part of your rib cage between the chest and abdominal cavities). Only the hand on your diaphragm should move with your breathing. If your other hand moves it means you're breathing from your chest. Dogs breathe diaphragmatically, and so do you if you get down on all fours. Practice *panting* in that position to strengthen your diaphragm.

Breathing Exercises

Before you do any voice exercises it's vital to relax your throat to avoid any strain on your voice. Keep your throat open and relaxed by yawning continually through exercises. For a stronger voice with better tone, breathe correctly and do the following exercises.

- Inhale and say *ah* on the exhaled breath.
- Put an *h* in front of the vowels *a e i o u,* and keep your throat open and relaxed.

Exercises to Develop Resonance

- Slide from one sound to the other—hm-bahhn-dahah (Only the sound *m, n,* and *ng* should go through the nose).
- Crying, crooning, moaning like the wind.
- Mumbo, jumbo, will hoo doo you.
- Blow wind by the lonely mound.
- Ah, moon of my delight that knows no wane.
- Sing oh ye muses now forevermore.
- Bring to the darkened hills the dawn of day.
- Ho ho he, ho he he, ho he hay, ho he hay haw, ho he hay haw ho.

Exercises to Overcome Nasality

Many voices are nasal, which is unpleasant to the ear. As only the sounds *n, m,* and *ng* should go through the nose, place your fingers lightly on your nostrils while you say *more, now,* and *going.* If you feel a vibration on any sounds but the *m,* and *ng* your voice is nasal.

- Say "She sang seventeen songs and swooned, woe, oh woe, oh woe!" with no nasality.
- An open and relaxed throat plus deep diaphragmatic breathing will help you overcome both nasality and a high tone. A high voice often lacks authority.

Your voice can either be a defect or an asset to your personality.

Bibliography

Allen, James. *As a Man Thinketh*. New York: Putnam Publishing Group, 1959.

Butler, Jessie Haver. *Time to Speak Up*. New York: Harper and Brothers, 1957.

Carnegie, Dale. *How to Win Friends and Influence People*. New York: Simon and Schuster, 1981.

Desfosses, Beatrice. *Your Voice and Your Speech*. New York: A. A. Wyn, 1946.

Fast, Julius. *Body Language*. New York: M. Evans and Company, 1970.

Flesch, Rudolph. *The Art of Clear Thinking*. New York: Harper and Row, 1951.

_____. *The Art of Plain Talk*. New York: Harper and Row, 1946.

Frank, Milo. *How to Get Your Point Across in 30 Seconds*. New York: Simon and Schuster, 1986.

Funk, Wilfred with Norman Lewis. *Six Weeks to Words of Power*. New York: Pocket Books, 1955.

_____. *30 Days to a More Powerful Vocabulary*. New York: Pocket Books, 1971.

Hayakawa, S. I. *Language in Thought and Action*. New York: Harcourt, Brace and World, 1964.

Hibbs, P., S. Fessenden, P. M. Larson, and J. A. Wagner. *Speech for Today*. New York: Webster McGraw-Hill, 1965.

Leeds, Dorothy. *Powerspeak*. New York: Prentice Hall Press, 1988.

Leedy, Paul. *Reading Improvement for Adults*. New York: McGraw-Hill, 1956.

Lewis, Norman. *Word Power Made Easy*. New York: Pocket Books, 1967.

McLuhan, Marshall. *Understanding Media. The Extensions of Man*. New York: McGraw-Hill, 1965.

Mares, Colin. *Rapid and Efficient Reading*. New York: Emerson Books, 1967.

Moncur, John P., and Harrison M. Karr. *Developing Your Speaking Voice*. New York, Evanston, San Francisco, London: Harper and Row, 1972.

Morris, William. *Your Heritage of Words*. New York: Dell Publishing Company, 1970.

Osgood, Charles. *Osgood on Speaking*. New York: William Morrow and Company, Inc., 1988.

Peale Norman Vincent. *The Amazing Results of Positive Thinking*. New York: Fawcett Crest, 1965. Ballantine Books Edition, 1982.

Pinckert, Robert C. *Pinckert's Practical Grammar*. Cincinnati, Ohio: Writer's Digest Books, 1986.

Reader's Digest. *How to Increase Your Word Power*. Cincinnati, Ohio: Reader's Digest, 1987.

Rizzo, Raymond. *The Voice as an Instrument*. New York: Bobbs-Merrill Company, 1969.

Sarnoff, Dorothy. *Speech Can Change Your Life*. New York: Doubleday and Company, Inc., 1970.

———. *Never Be Nervous Again*. New York: Crown Publishers, 1987.

Shrope, Wayne Austin. *Speaking and Listening*. New York: Harcourt, Brace and World, 1970.

Walters, Barbara. *How to Talk with Practically Anybody about Practically Anything*. New York: Doubleday and Company, 1970.